YOU CHOOSE
BOOKS
Historical Eras

The Middle Ages

An Interactive History Adventure

by Allison Lassieur

Consultant:
Phillip C. Adamo
Associate Professor of History and
Director of Medieval Studies
Augsburg College
Minneapolis, Minnesota

Capstone
press

Mankato, Minnesota

You Choose Books are published by Capstone Press,
1710 Roe Crest Drive, North Mankato, Minnesota 56003.
www.capstonepub.com

Books published by Capstone Press are manufactured with paper
containing at least 10 percent post-consumer waste.

Library of Congress Cataloging-in-Publication Data
Lassieur, Allison.
 The Middle Ages : an interactive history adventure / by Allison Lassieur.
 p. cm. — (You choose: historical eras)
 Includes bibliographical references and index.
 Summary: "Describes the life and times of the era known as the Middle Ages. The reader's
choices reveal the historical details of life as a knight in the 1100s, life in a royal castle in the
1200s, and life during the Black Plague in the 1300s" — Provided by publisher.
 ISBN 978-1-4296-3418-2 (library binding)   ISBN 978-1-4296-3908-8 (pbk.)
 1. Middle Ages — Juvenile literature. I. Title.
D117.L376 2010
940.1 — dc22   2008054998

Editorial Credits

Jennifer Besel, editor; Juliette Peters, set designer; Veronica Bianchini, book designer;
 Wanda Winch, media researcher

Photo Credits

The Art Archive/Saint Sebastian Chapel Lanslevillard Savoy/Gianni Dagli Orti, 86; Art
Resource, N.Y./Scala, 50; The Bridgeman Art Library/Giraudon/The Taking of Tripoli,
April 1102, by Charles Alexandre Debacq, (1804-50)/Chateau de Versailles, France, 63; The
Bridgeman Art Library/Giraudon/View of the Town Hall, Marseilles, during the Plague of 1720,
detail of the carts laden with the dead (oil on canvas) (detail of 52281), Serre, Michel (1658-
1753) / Musee des Beaux-Arts, Marseille, France, 90; The Bridgeman Art Library/© Look and
Learn/Private Collection/The Black Death, English School, 95; The Bridgeman Art Library/©
Look and Learn/Private Collection/The Black Death (gouache on paper), Nicolle, Pat (Patrick)
(1907-95), 75; The Bridgeman Art Library/National Library, St. Petersburg, Russia/Ms Lat.
Q.v.I.126 f.79v Burial Procession, from the "Book of Hours of Louis d'Orleans", 1469, Colombe,
Jean (c.1430-c.93), 97; great-castles.com/Ron Lyons Jr., 21; Mary Evans Picture Library, 64, 80,
104; North Wind Picture Archives, cover, 6, 12, 18, 57, 66, 70; Peter Newark's Historical Pictures,
38, 40, 100; Peter Newark's Military Pictures, 15, 25, 32, 45

Printed in the United States of America in Stevens Point, Wisconsin.
032012   006660R

TABLE OF CONTENTS

ABOUT YOUR ADVENTURE

YOU live during the late Middle Ages. War and plague are everywhere. Even everyday life is hard. Will you survive?

In this book, you'll explore how the choices people made meant the difference between life and death. The events you'll experience happened to real people.

Chapter One sets the scene. Then you choose which path to read. Follow the directions at the bottom of each page. The choices you make will change your outcome. After you finish one path, go back and read the others for new perspectives and more adventures.

*YOU CHOOSE the path
you take through history.*

Large castles were built for royalty during the Middle Ages.

Castles, War, and Plague

Historians label the years between about 500 and 1500 the Middle Ages. This time is called the Middle Ages because it is between the ancient and the modern periods of history.

Stories about the Middle Ages are filled with excitement and battles. Grand kings and queens ruled their subjects. Knights bravely fought great battles. Castles stood tall on hillsides.

Real life in the Middle Ages was not all glory and gold, though. It was a complicated time, just like any other period in history. Some of the kings and queens were cruel. War and disease killed many people.

Turn the page.

At that time, the people were basically divided into three orders, or ways of life. There were those who fought, those who prayed, and those who worked. In this society, everyone had a role that served the other orders.

The people who fought included the knights. The knights promised to protect the poor and the weak. Wealthy nobles allowed their knights to use land in exchange for a promise to fight when asked.

The second order was people of religion, such as priests and monks. Their job was to pray for everyone. This was important because most people believed strongly in the reward of heaven and the punishment of hell.

The third order included all the workers. The farmers and the peasants worked the fields and grew food for everyone.

Warfare was a huge part of life in the Middle Ages, and the biggest wars were the Crusades. This series of wars was fought between Christians and Muslims. They were mainly fighting over the city of Jerusalem, located in present-day Israel. Christians believed Jerusalem was the holiest city. Muslims also considered Jerusalem holy to their faith. And the Muslims had lived there for hundreds of years and considered it their home.

The area around Jerusalem was called the Holy Land. Christians believed they should rule the Holy Land. Of course, Muslims did not believe Christians had any right to take their land. For 200 years, thousands of knights and soldiers fought the Crusades. The Christian soldiers hoped to take the Holy Land away from the Muslims.

Turn the page.

The Crusades were only one part of life in the Middle Ages. Ordinary people spent most of their lives in small villages or towns on a noble's fiefdom. Most people were farmers, but others worked as blacksmiths, weavers, glassmakers, and metalsmiths. Stone carvers and woodworkers traveled from town to town, looking for work building castles or cathedrals.

In 1347, a horrifying sickness called the Black Plague began to sweep through Europe. No one knows exactly how many people died. But whole towns lost their populations. People dropped dead in city streets. To the people of the Middle Ages, it seemed like the end of the world.

The Middle Ages lasted for about 1,000 years.

Many people lived and died during this time.

And they all had very different experiences.

➤ To fight battles as a knight in the 1100s, turn to page **13**.

➤ To explore life in a royal castle in the 1200s, turn to page **41**.

➤ To experience the terror of the Black Plague in the 1300s, turn to page **67**.

During the Middle Ages, squires helped knights prepare for battle as part of their training.

CHAPTER 2

Honor and Chivalry

It is springtime in England in the year 1190. You are an eager young squire to your cousin, a well-known knight named Sir Henry. Six years ago, when you were 12, your parents sent you to live with Sir Henry and his family. You want nothing more than to be a great knight like your cousin.

Every day, you have lessons in sword fighting. You practice horseback riding. You also clean Sir Henry's armor and weapons. When you are not training in the field, you learn to read and write. You memorize the songs and stories that fill the feast hall at night. You attend church services each day, because above all, a knight must love God.

Turn the page.

Now you are 18 years old. One day, Sir Henry summons you to his chambers.

"Are you ready to become a knight?" he asks.

"Yes," you reply, your heart pounding.

"You are a worthy squire," says Sir Henry. "You shall become a knight."

That evening, Sir Henry and several nobles lead you to a room that holds a large wooden tub. Steam rises from the warm water.

"The first part of the knighting ritual is a bath," Sir Henry explains. "The bath symbolizes the washing away of your sins."

After your bath, Sir Henry and the nobles take you to the castle chapel. "You will stay here all night, praying about the decision you've made," Sir Henry says. You kneel on the hard, cold stone for many hours.

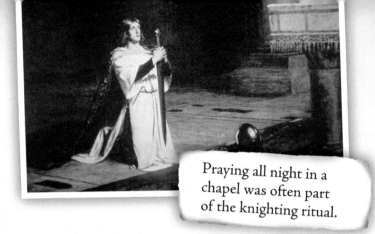

Praying all night in a chapel was often part of the knighting ritual.

At dawn, the men return, and a crowd gathers in the chapel. Sir Henry buckles a new sword around your waist.

"Is it your wish to serve God and the land as a knight?" he asks in a deep voice. "And do you promise to defend all ladies and to always treat them with respect?"

"Yes," you reply.

15

Sir Henry steps closer. "Now I will dub you." Sir Henry reaches out and slaps your face. "From this day forward, let no blow go unanswered, in the name of honor and chivalry."

Turn the page.

Everyone moves to the great hall, where a delicious feast is waiting.

As you eat, Sir Henry leans toward you. "I am going on Crusade," he says.

Crusade! King Richard the Lion-Hearted is about to lead an army to the Holy Land. The Holy Land is controlled by Arab Muslims. Richard, along with the kings of France and Germany, has vowed to take the Holy Land back from the Muslims.

"I want to go on Crusade with you," you say excitedly.

"You can if you wish," Sir Henry replies. "But I also need someone I trust to stay here and protect my lands."

→ To stay behind and guard Sir Henry's lands, go to page 17.

→ To go on Crusade, turn to page 19.

It is an honor that Sir Henry trusts you to protect his lands, so you agree to stay. Each morning, you ride through the castle grounds. In the afternoon, you practice sword fighting. Once a week, the local peasants come to the castle. You settle disputes and give permission for marriages.

One day, a knight appears in the hall. "Greetings, my friend Arthur," you say. Then you notice the worried expression on his face. "What is the matter?"

"William Longchamp, the chancellor of England, is marching toward Gerard de Camville's castle with an army," he says. "Longchamp plans to attack Lincoln Castle. King Richard's brother, Prince John, is against Longchamp's move."

Turn the page.

Before he had left on Crusade, King Richard appointed Longchamp chancellor. But you have heard that Longchamp is abusing his power.

"But Prince John wants to be king, and he might support anyone who will help him get power," Sir Arthur says. "Both men are calling for your help."

Which one deserves your support?

Many people did not trust Prince John because they thought he was trying to steal power.

→ To side with Prince John and defend Lincoln Castle, turn to page **20**.

→ To join Longchamp in the attack, turn to page **22**.

"King Richard's crusaders sail from France in the summer," Sir Henry says. "We will cross down through France and meet Richard's army in Marseilles." After many hurried preparations, you set out.

Crossing the English Channel is exciting. But once you're in France, you have days of horseback riding ahead of you. You quickly tire of being in the saddle all day. One evening, you and Sir Henry find a small inn. It doesn't look very clean, but you're both exhausted. You're also hungry.

"I have some stew," the innkeeper says.

Sir Henry glances at the stew. "Be careful. It might not be wise to eat strange food."

The stew smells so good. And you're tired of eating bread and cheese every day.

➤ To take Sir Henry's advice, turn to page **26**.

➤ To eat the stew, turn to page **39**.

Longchamp has no right to attack Lincoln Castle. You must help defend it. Quickly, you ride to the castle. You fear that you will be too late. But Longchamp's army is not there when you arrive.

"I am Nicholaa de Camville," a young, strong woman says as she greets you. "I am lady of this castle. My lord husband, Gerard de Camville, is not here. He is away with Prince John now. It is up to us to defend Lincoln Castle. I am grateful you have come to help us."

A few hours later, Longchamp's army rumbles toward the castle. As you watch the army approach, Lady Nicholaa comes to you.

"I need fighters to defend the castle from the inside," she says. "But I also need brave knights to ride out and meet the army."

Lincoln Castle still stands in England today.

→ To defend the castle from inside, turn to page **24**.

→ To ride out to meet the army, turn to page **33**.

Longchamp has King Richard's trust, and that is enough for you. The next day, you ride to Longchamp's army, which is camped a few miles from the castle. When you arrive, you go to his tent.

Longchamp smiles. "All help is welcome," he says.

Early the next morning, the army prepares for the march to Lincoln Castle. Longchamp appears, riding a fine battle horse.

"We will win the day!" he cries. "I need good soldiers to march in the front ranks and attack the castle. But my greatest need will be strong guards to protect the war machine. We'll use a trebuchet to throw boulders into the castle walls. But the machine has to be protected in order for the men to load the boulders."

→ To march out in front, turn to page **30**.

→ To guard the war machine, turn to page **34**.

"I will stay here with your men," you say.

"Very well," Lady Nicholaa says. "You will command the forces along the wall."

Soon Longchamp's army is in position. Their metal armor glints in the sun. As you watch from the castle wall, Longchamp's soldiers move a trebuchet toward the castle. It is a huge wooden machine with a long arm. A big sling is attached to the arm. Soldiers load a boulder into the sling. When the arm is released, it can throw the boulder hundreds of feet.

But your army is ready for them. "Archers!" you shout, raising your sword. "Ready! Fire!" A cloud of arrows zooms over the tower wall and rains down. The screams from below tell you that the volley was successful.

Suddenly someone near you screams, "Run!" You look up to see a huge boulder flying through the air. "It must have come from the trebuchet," you think. It's your last thought as the boulder slams into the wall, throwing you to your death.

The trebuchet was a powerful weapon during battles.

THE END

To follow another path, turn to page 11.
To read the conclusion, turn to page 101.

As good as the stew smells, you decide not to eat. You can't trust that the food is safe. The next morning, you nibble on bread and cheese as you and Sir Henry continue on.

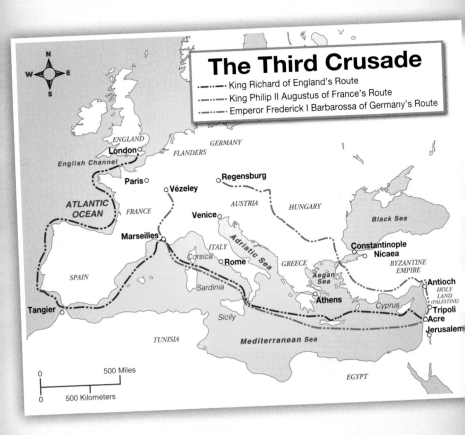

The Third Crusade

---·—·— King Richard of England's Route
---·—·— King Philip II Augustus of France's Route
---·—·— Emperor Frederick I Barbarossa of Germany's Route

Finally you arrive in Marseilles, the oldest city in France. Marseilles has become an important trading post. The port is full of ships carrying goods from Asia and other faraway places.

Hundreds of crusaders crowd the docks. They are waiting to board the ships that will take them to the Holy Land. As you wait, a tall, athletic man rides toward you on a magnificent horse. He stops to greet Sir Henry.

"Your majesty, King Richard," Sir Henry says, bowing. Shocked, you bow too.

"So this is the young knight I have heard of," the king says, smiling at you. "We need all good knights if we are to recapture the Holy Land."

Turn the page.

After a few delays, the ships set sail. When the army arrives in Sicily, you expect you will quickly continue on to the Holy Land. But the army makes camp and waits. After several days, you find out what has caused the delay. The ruler of Sicily, Tancred of Lecce, refused to give Richard the ships and supplies he had promised.

To your disappointment, the army is stuck in Sicily for the whole winter. It isn't until spring 1191 that Richard's army can finally move on.

One morning, Sir Henry comes to you and says, "The king is calling for good knights to take a special assignment. He needs royal guards to sail with his fiancée, Berengaria, and his sister, Queen Joanna of Sicily. I have volunteered. Would you like to join me?"

Guarding the future queen of England is an honor. But it sounds dull. What do you do?

➤ To guard the future queen, turn to page **31**.

➤ To refuse the offer, turn to page **36**.

From your spot at the front of the army, you can see that Lincoln Castle is well protected. Soldiers and archers line the walls above you.

Slowly Longchamp's huge war machine, the trebuchet, rumbles forward. The trebuchet can hurl a large boulder hundreds of feet. You doubt the castle wall can withstand a trebuchet attack.

A shout comes from the castle walls. You look up to see a cloud of arrows coming down. Before you can raise your shield, an arrow pierces your neck. You feel the warm blood flowing beneath your armor as you fall. You die there on the dusty ground.

THE END

To follow another path, turn to page 11.
To read the conclusion, turn to page 101.

"Of course I will join you," you say. Soon the fleet sails away.

Strong storms batter the ships and scatter the fleet. Instead of guarding the future queen, you spend most of your time seasick in your hammock below deck. You hear that on another ship, King Richard is also very seasick.

The storms force your ship to dock in Cyprus. There you hear some bad news. Some of the other ships in the fleet wrecked in the storms. The emperor of Cyprus, Isaac Dukas Comnenus, has taken many of the shipwrecked survivors hostage.

A few days later, King Richard's ship arrives. You rejoice that the king survived the storms. But King Richard is not pleased that the emperor has taken his men hostage.

Turn the page.

Sir Henry finds you. "Richard's ambassadors asked the emperor to let the men go," he says. "But the emperor refused. Prepare for battle!"

Dozens of small boats filled with soldiers head to shore. When you reach land, you rush forward with a shout. Many of the emperor's men are fighting King Richard's soldiers along the shore. But some of the emperor's soldiers are fleeing toward the town.

Crusaders fought hard, believing that they fought for God.

→ To chase the emperor's soldiers, turn to page 37.

→ To stay on the shore and fight, turn to page 38.

"I will face this army!" you shout. Soon you and a handful of soldiers are galloping toward the oncoming army. Longchamp's soldiers and knights are ready for you. There is a clash of metal as the two armies meet. You rush forward, slashing and cutting with your sword.

A sharp pain in your shoulder makes you spin around. A knight in full armor is about to strike you again. Quickly you swing your sword upward and deflect the blow.

Above the noise of the fighting you hear a trumpet call. Then someone yells, "Retreat! Retreat!" Longchamp's soldiers turn and flee from the castle wall. You join the other soldiers in a ragged cheer as the enemy runs. You're glad the fighting is over, at least for now.

THE END

To follow another path, turn to page 11.
To read the conclusion, turn to page 101.

Guarding the machine isn't glorious, but it is an important job. The men who operate the machine are the first targets for the enemy.

The army approaches Lincoln Castle and stops. A large number of soldiers begin pulling the trebuchet forward.

Several enemy soldiers rush toward the trebuchet as the men load a huge boulder into the sling on the machine. Your sword flashes in the sun as you fight to keep the enemies away. With a shout, your men let go of the rope holding the arm of the trebuchet. The arm flies upward, tossing the boulder into the air. The boulder hits the castle wall with a mighty crash. The soldiers in the castle scatter.

As the battle continues, you bravely fight any enemy who dares attack the trebuchet.

Finally a trumpet sounds from behind you. "Retreat!" Longchamp shouts.

"Why are we retreating?" you call to Longchamp as he gallops past you.

"De Camville wants to talk with me," Longchamp says. "Maybe she will surrender!"

If de Camville surrenders, you can go home. If not, there will be another battle to fight tomorrow.

THE END

To follow another path, turn to page 11.
To read the conclusion, turn to page 101.

35

"I will leave the honor of guarding the future queen to you," you tell Sir Henry.

You set sail with the other knights, but this isn't like the first part of the trip. There is stormy weather every day. The ship rolls and twists on the waves, and you're seasick and miserable. The journey seems to go on forever. One afternoon, an enormous storm hits. "We're going down!" someone yells. "Abandon ship!"

Wave after wave crashes onto the deck. One monstrous wave carries you into the sea. The freezing water quickly fills your lungs, and you gasp for breath. You drown in the sea, far from home.

THE END

To follow another path, turn to page 11.
To read the conclusion, turn to page 101.

Yelling, you run for the fleeing soldiers. Without warning, several of the emperor's men appear, swords drawn. They all attack you at once, shouting in a language you don't understand. At first you fight hard. But the long journey and seasickness affected you. You are too slow, and a soldier strikes you. A searing pain rips through your stomach. You drop to your knees. For you, the great adventure of the Crusades is over as you die thousands of miles from home.

THE END

To follow another path, turn to page 11.
To read the conclusion, turn to page 101.

King Richard spent most of his time as king fighting wars.

Running forward, you swing your sword at the first enemy soldier you see on the shore. He turns and strikes with his sword. You block it with your shield and thrust your sword into his neck. Screaming, the man falls to the ground.

Before you know it, the battle is over. The shore is littered with bodies, and the sand is stained red. You fall to your knees and thank God for King Richard's success in Cyprus. You're not sure what will happen next. But you are confident Richard's army will reclaim the Holy Land.

THE END

To follow another path, turn to page 11.
To read the conclusion, turn to page 101.

38

You're sick of bread and cheese. The innkeeper hands you a bowl of stew. You wolf it down. After thanking her, you go to your room for the night.

The next day, you and Sir Henry continue traveling. You don't feel right all morning. Your mouth goes dry, and your eyelids start to droop. Your speech becomes slurred, and you have trouble staying on your horse. Sir Henry makes camp as you curl miserably in front of the fire.

"God must be punishing me for something I did," you think sadly. You grow weaker, and it becomes hard to breathe. By morning, you are dead.

39

THE END

To follow another path, turn to page 11.
To read the conclusion, turn to page 101.

Visitors can still explore Leeds Castle in England.

CHAPTER 3

Life in the Castle

It is 1279, and Edward I is king of England. His wife is Queen Eleanor of Castile, who is beautiful and kind. Your mother is a lady-in-waiting to the queen. Your mother's main job is to take care of the queen's jewelry. But she does whatever the queen needs. It is a great honor to be a lady-in-waiting. One day, you'd like to have that job too.

Now, though, you live in Leeds Castle with the families of other nobles who work for the king. People say that King Edward plans to build many more castles. You doubt they will be as beautiful as Leeds.

Turn the page.

The king and queen travel a great deal, and their staff travels with them. The queen has been traveling for many weeks, and your mother is with her. You miss your mother.

Your father is the steward of Leeds Castle. He is in charge of the entire household. It's one of the most important jobs in the castle.

One evening, Father comes to you. "I have just received word that the queen is arriving at Leeds Castle in two days," he says with a smile.

"Mother is coming home!" you shout.

"There is a small group of people who are going out to meet the queen," Father says. "I must stay here and prepare the castle for her arrival. I could use your help. But if you want to go out with the escort, that is fine too."

→ To stay and help Father, go to page **43**.

→ To leave with the escort, turn to page **46**.

"If you need my help, Father, I will stay," you say.

"Wonderful," he says. "We'll start in the morning."

The next day, you wake up and wash your face in the basin. You pull on a gown and neatly braid your hair. Then you slide your feet into your soft leather slippers. Quickly, you run to the steward's office.

"There you are!" Father says. "I have so much for you to do today. I need to get a message to Sir Robert. I think he is training this morning. I also must get the menu for the queen's first dinner from the master cook."

➺ To go to the training field, turn to page 44.

➺ To go to the royal kitchens, turn to page 48.

You dash through the main courtyard toward the field. You wave to Katherine, the head laundress, and her maids as they carry large buckets of water to the laundry. The stable hands are busy cleaning out the horse stalls. You avoid the steaming manure piles as you pass.

Soon you are out of the castle gate. You follow the sounds of shouting and the clashing of metal swords. Sir Robert and a group of young squires are on the training field.

"My lady, well met!" Sir Robert says when he sees you. "Have you come to learn to fight?"

"Not today," you say with a smile. "The queen is coming!" You hand him the message from your father.

Sir Robert reads the note and then says, "Tell your father I will do as he asks. But can you do something for me?"

He points to his tunic, which has several tears in it. "A young squire got a bit too excited during practice," he says. "Will you go to the tailor and tell him to begin making me a new one?"

Squires practiced for war before they could become knights.

➤ To go to the tailor, turn to page **50**.

➤ To return to your father, turn to page **53**.

The next day, the castle's courtyard is crowded with horses and wagons being readied for the escort. Luggage, barrels of food and drink, and many other things are loaded onto several wagons. The royal guards wear colorful tunics and matching cloaks. The king's banners flutter in the morning breeze.

You are given a pony to ride. All the horses, including yours, are covered with golden trappings. Colorful ribbons are braided into their manes.

The escort sets off. "Good-bye, Father!" you shout.

"Be safe!" he shouts in reply.

Bells on the wagons jingle softly as the group moves slowly through the countryside. Your pony is lively and restless. You try to control him, but it's not easy.

"Are you having trouble?" a voice calls. You look up to see Sir Walter Beauchamp, a knight and one of the king's friends.

"A little," you admit, pulling on the reins.

"Why don't you ride in the cart for a bit?" Sir Walter suggests. "Your pony might calm down."

➤ To stay on the pony, turn to page **52**.

➤ To ride in the cart, turn to page **56**.

The kitchens are hot and crowded. Several servants roughly push by you, glaring at you as they pass.

"Sorry," you mumble.

You watch two boys struggle to cut a large hunk of meat on one table. You don't see the dairymaid rush in, carrying two baskets of fresh eggs. She runs right into you, and the eggs spill out onto the stone floor with a loud crunch.

"Now look what you've done!" the girl cries, dropping to her knees to clean up the mess. "What are you doing in here?"

"I'm sorry," you say, bending down to help her. "I'm looking for the master cook."

"She's over by the fireplace," the girl says as you help her wipe up the broken eggs. "Now get out of here before you make more trouble!"

You finally find the cook, grinding spices in a huge stone mortar. A fire is roaring in the fireplace, and several large pots hang above it.

"You must be here for the menu," she says, wiping her hands on her gown. "Tell your father I will prepare the queen's favorites. There will be venison with pepper sauce, mushrooms and leeks, and fried fish in wine and onion broth. I will also serve custard tarts with fruit, yellow cake, nuts, breads, cheeses, and spiced wine."

You nod, your mouth watering. The cook sees how hungry she's made you. "I could use a hand in here today, if you have some time. I might have some leftovers for you to sample."

Turn to page 53.

"Of course," you say, bowing to Sir Robert.

Charles the tailor works in a large room with several windows. Bolts of colorful cloth are stacked high against one wall. A long wooden table is covered with pieces of cut cloth.

"Ah, and how are you today?" Charles asks as you walk in. "Is it time for a new gown?"

Tailors sewed colorful clothing for the rich during the Middle Ages.

"No, not today," you reply. You give Charles the message from Sir Robert. He frowns.

"That man goes through more linen tunics than the king, and that's saying something," Charles says. "Very well. It will be done."

As you leave, you see your best friend, Agnes. Her father is the head of the stables. "There's a litter of kittens in the stables," Agnes says excitedly. "Want to come see them with me?"

"I don't know," you say. "Father is counting on me to help him today."

"Oh, but they are so cute!" Agnes says. "You must come!"

➤ *To go back to your father, turn to page 53.*

➤ *To go with Agnes, turn to page 57.*

"I can handle him," you say stubbornly. Sir Walter nods and trots ahead on his horse.

Suddenly a rabbit bursts out of the bushes and dashes across the road. Your pony rears and gallops into the forest.

"Help!" you cry as you crash through the underbrush. A branch catches your shoulder, and you fall to the ground. You feel a terrible pain in your leg.

Sir Walter and several others rush to you. "You are injured," he says gravely. "You must go back to the castle immediately."

"But I don't want to go back," you say, wincing at the pain.

"It is your choice," Sir Walter replies.

→ To go back to the castle, turn to page 58.

→ To stay with the escort, turn to page 61.

"I'm sorry, but I need to help my father today," you say as you head back to the steward's office.

"Taking your time, eh?" Father says jokingly when you return. Then he becomes serious and says, "I have several other things for you to do. Stay alert and return as fast as you can. There is much for us to do today."

"Yes, Father," you say.

You spend the afternoon running errands and delivering items to people throughout the castle. As evening comes, you stop by the hall for something to eat, and then you go to your rooms.

You've never felt this tired! You pull off your gown, leaving your light linen undergown on for sleeping. You crawl between the sheets, the straw mattress rustling beneath you. "Mother is coming home tomorrow," you think as you drift off to sleep.

Turn the page.

You awake to the sound of trumpet blasts. The queen is coming! Quickly you dress and rush down to the courtyard. It is packed with people, all yelling and shouting for the queen. You climb to the top of a wall just as the great wooden castle gates grind open. The crowd cheers as the royal guards appear, their colorful banners fluttering in the breeze. Behind them, the queen and her ladies ride in the back of an elegant wagon. You wave wildly, screaming, "Long live the queen!"

As soon as they pass, you run inside the castle. "Mother, Mother!" you cry when you see the ladies-in-waiting. Your mother turns and grabs you in a strong hug. "I have missed you!" she says. Then you both turn and bow low as the queen approaches.

"I am so glad to see you," Queen Eleanor says, taking your hand. She is beautiful, with dark hair and dark eyes. She smiles at you. "Your mother speaks so highly of you," she says. "I think you'll be ready to work for me soon."

The queen turns and disappears into the castle, surrounded by her ladies-in-waiting. You smile as you watch her go, knowing that soon you'll be a lady-in-waiting, just like your mother.

THE END

To follow another path, turn to page 11.
To read the conclusion, turn to page 101.

"I think you are right," you say. You dismount and hand the reins to Sir Walter.

"Why don't you ride in the covered wagon with my wife, Alice?" he says.

Gratefully you climb into one of the brightly painted covered wagons where the noble ladies ride.

"Please join us," Alice says as they all make room for you. You get caught up in lively gossip about life in the royal court. Before you know it, the escort is stopping for the evening meal.

You grab buckets and head into the woods to fetch water from a clear spring. When you hear a rustling behind you, you turn. Two rough, dirty men dash out of the woods toward you.

➤ To freeze, turn to page 60.

➤ To try to run back to the escort, turn to page 62.

"All right," you say. But you've never liked the stables. The warhorses scare you. Agnes sees you shiver when you see the horses.

"Don't worry about the horses," she says. Agnes crawls under the stable door. You follow, glancing up at the biggest horse. His tail swishes wildly, and a whinny rumbles in his throat.

"I need to leave," you say, turning to run. Before you can move, the horse rears and kicks you. By the time you fall to the ground, you are unconscious. Soon after, you die of your injuries.

57

Knights rode large warhorses called chargers into battle.

THE END

To follow another path, turn to page 11.
To read the conclusion, turn to page 101.

By nightfall you are back in your bed at the castle. The pain is worse, and a fever grips you.

"The royal surgeon is with the queen," Father says worriedly, wiping your forehead. "They will be here soon. I will care for you until then."

By the next morning, your fever is raging. Father sends for a healing woman.

"Her leg is broken," she says. "I can set it. I will also make a medicine that will draw out the infection." She makes a thick paste out of comfrey root. She soaks strips of cloth in the paste, then wraps them around your leg. Then she puts a splint on your leg.

At first it hurts more, but soon the pain begins to fade. A few hours later, your fever breaks.

You know you're lucky to be alive. As you weakly nibble on a crust of bread, you hope that you are well enough to greet your mother when she arrives.

59

THE END

To follow another path, turn to page 11.
To read the conclusion, turn to page 101.

You freeze, hoping the men won't see you. But it doesn't work. The men grab you and put a nasty-looking dagger to your throat.

"A girl from the castle," one man says with a growl. "The king took my farm. My family died. Now he will pay with this girl!"

You struggle, but he tightens his grip. "Don't try to run. You will regret it."

His words only make you struggle harder. You kick him in the shin, and he howls with pain. You try to run. But you only make it a few steps before you feel a sharp pain in your side. Reaching, you feel the handle of the dagger.

"I'll never see Mother again," you think as you watch your blood spill onto the dusty ground.

THE END

To follow another path, turn to page 11.
To read the conclusion, turn to page 101.

You stay with the escort, but it doesn't take long to realize you've made a mistake. You get a raging fever, and your leg throbs. Sir Walter gently lays you in a wagon and covers you with a warm blanket.

"We will be at the royal encampment soon," he says. "The royal surgeon can help you then."

As the day wears on, your pain gets worse. You become unconscious from the pain and the fever. You barely notice when several people lift you out of the wagon and lay you on the ground next to a roaring fire. You try to drink some water, but you can't swallow. Sir Walter orders a guard to ride ahead and fetch the surgeon. But it is too late. By dawn, you are dead from an infection in your wounds.

THE END

To follow another path, turn to page 11.
To read the conclusion, turn to page 101.

"Help!" you scream, throwing the water bucket at the men. You run as fast as you can to Sir Walter.

"Outlaws," you gasp, pointing to the woods.

Instantly the knight and several others rush into the woods. You hear shouting and the clang of swords. Soon the men return.

"Those outlaws won't be bothering us again," Sir Walter says grimly, wiping blood from his sword. "Are you all right?"

You nod, shaking. Alice puts her arms around you. Soon you are warm and eating a hot supper near a roaring campfire.

The next afternoon, the escort arrives at the royal encampment. Your eyes widen in wonder at the sight. Dozens of bright, colorful tents are set up in a large clearing, surrounded by many wagons. People hurry back and forth, carrying food, boxes, and baskets. Hunks of meat sizzle on spits, and hot cauldrons of delicious-smelling food bubble over several fires.

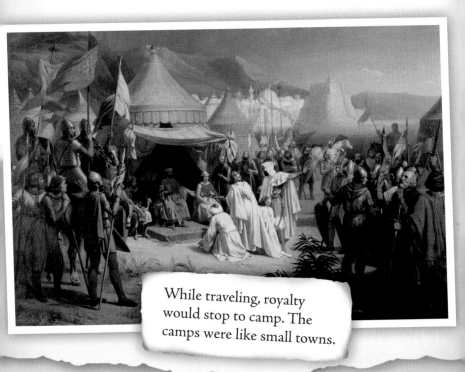

While traveling, royalty would stop to camp. The camps were like small towns.

Turn the page.

You can tell the queen's tent because it is the largest and most beautiful. As you run toward it, your mother comes out.

"My dear!" she cries, folding you into her arms. "I have missed you so!"

Queen Eleanor of Castile cared deeply for her ladies-in-waiting and their families.

Another woman comes out of the tent. You immediately recognize Queen Eleanor. She is beautiful, with dark hair and eyes. She wears a rich gown of green silk covered in embroidery and jewels. She bends to hug you too.

You follow the two women into the royal tent. Inside it is filled with a heavy wooden bed, chairs, cushions, tables, and even carpets on the ground! One table is set with silver plates piled with fruit. As your mother attends the queen, you sink onto a cushion. You're glad your adventure is over for now.

65

THE END

To follow another path, turn to page 11.
To read the conclusion, turn to page 101.

Before the plague hit, Florence, Italy, was a bustling town.

CHAPTER 4

The Black Death

It is 1348, and you are living in Florence, Italy. Many say that Florence is the grandest city in Italy, and you agree. The sparkling Arno River flows through the city. Tall buildings rise above the cobblestone streets.

You grew up in this beautiful city and became an apprentice to a woodcarver when you were only 8 years old. Now you are a master carver with a shop of your own. It is a small shop in the market district of Florence.

As you enter your shop this fine morning, you look around. Everything is covered with a layer of sawdust. Several projects lean against the walls, covered with white cloths. Your apprentice, Sebastian, is already hard at work on a crucifix for the local church.

Turn the page.

"Good morning, master," Sebastian says. "Someone named Andrea was here already this morning. He wants us to carve a statue for the new church. Also, Leonardo came by. He said that the wood you ordered is ready."

"I'll go out to take care of those things," you tell Sebastian. "I may be gone all day. Lock the shop when you leave."

"There's one more thing," Sebastian says. "I have heard troubling news from Sicily. There is talk that many people are dying there of a terrible sickness."

"I would not worry," you say. "Sicily is far away. Surely no sickness could get through the mighty walls of Florence!" With that, you walk out of the shop.

➠ To find Andrea at the church, go to page **69**.

➠ To get the wood from Leonardo, turn to page **72**.

You step into the narrow street and walk toward the church. The street is already busy at this early hour. People stop in front of stalls and counters to buy hot sausages and to exchange news and gossip. You hear your name and turn to see your friend Antonio in the crowd.

"What news?" you ask.

"There is rumor of sickness," he says nervously. "I have a friend who lives near the edge of town. He says that many graves have been dug these past few days."

You can't believe it. "He must be mistaken," you say confidently.

Antonio shrugs. "I hope so," he says.

You bid him good-bye and push your way through the city streets.

Turn the page.

Up ahead you see the new cathedral. It is still under construction, and the sound of hammers fills the air as you approach. You pick your way through the construction site until you see a familiar face.

"Ah, my friend!" Andrea Pisano shouts over the noise.

You spend some time talking about the job he wants you to do.

The Cathedral of Santa Maria del Fiore in Florence was finished after the plague.

"I am honored that you would choose me to carve the statues," you tell Andrea.

"Well, I must return to Orvieto, where I am building another cathedral," he says. Then he leans toward you. "I don't want to be in town if this sickness arrives," he says. "Orvieto is a small town. I will be safer there, I think."

"If this sickness is as bad as they say, there will be no place of safety," you reply. "But I do not think it will be that bad."

"I hope not," Andrea says. "Good-bye, my friend."

"Be well," you say. You told Andrea the sickness won't be bad. But deep down, you're getting nervous.

➤ To finish your errands, turn to page 73.

➤ To return to your shop, turn to page 77.

Leonardo is a woodcutter who lives outside the city. As you pass the gate, a guard stops you.

"Are you leaving Florence?" he asks gruffly.

Surprised, you say, "What business is it of yours?"

"We are closing the gates soon," he says, "to keep out the sickness."

Now you are very worried. "I will be back before you close the gates," you say, and you hurry on. Soon you come to Leonardo's home. You expect to hear the sound of sawing, but all is quiet.

"Leonardo?" you call. You push open the door and go inside. The table is set as if someone were about to eat a meal. But no one is here.

➤ To search the house, turn to page **76**.

➤ To turn and go home, turn to page **77**.

You set off to finish your errands. Women lean out windows, calling to one another as they hang their wash on long poles. A group of soldiers ride by on fine horses. Then you hear a sound that breaks through the everyday noises of Florence. Two crying women spill out of a doorway as three men carry a shrouded body into the street. Everyone on the street pauses as the body is carried away.

"It is the sickness," people whisper.

"No," others say. "It will not come here."

The sight of the dead body and the weeping women would not normally be disturbing. After all, people die in a city every day. But with all the talk of a terrible sickness, you become uneasy. You want to finish your errands and get back home.

Turn the page.

First you stop at the cobblers, where you pick up a pair of shoes you had left to be repaired.

"Good thing you came today," the cobbler says, handing you the shoes. "I am leaving tomorrow. Maybe I will be spared." You feel a pain in your chest as you leave. You ignore it, thinking it's nothing.

Your next stop is the wool merchant's shop. But the door is locked, and no one answers. "They have not been seen for a few days," one of the neighbors tells you. You decide it's time to go home.

As you walk through the streets, a fit of coughing overcomes you. You are horrified to see that you're coughing up blood. Until this moment you were fine, but suddenly you are dizzy and weak. You stumble and fall to the ground, covered in blood.

You expect someone to help. But instead, a crowd gathers around you. "The sickness," they say. "It is the plague!"

Your head swims, and you cough up more blood as you try to catch your breath. The people step back, then run away quickly. You die alone in the street.

The plague swept through cities and towns. People dropped dead in the streets.

THE END

To follow another path, turn to page 11.
To read the conclusion, turn to page 101.

Slowly you move through the house. No one is in the front room or in the first bedroom. Everything is neat and orderly, as if Leonardo had simply stepped out for a moment. You push open a third door, and a horrifying sight greets you. Leonardo and his wife are lying in bed in a pool of blood. The smell of death is everywhere.

You back away, gagging.

"How can this be?" you think. "He just came to my shop this morning!" You shut the door and run out of the house. This sickness is truly terrible.

When you arrive back at your shop, Sebastian is gone. That evening, you hear a knock on the door.

"My friend!" a voice calls. "Are you well?" It is your good friend Giovanni Boccaccio. "I am well. You don't have to fear me!"

You unlock the door and let him in. "I am so glad you are not sick," you say.

He nods. "People are dying everywhere. The church graveyards are too full to take more of the dead. They have started digging pits to hold the bodies." Giovanni grips your shoulder. "Many people are fleeing the city," he says. "They say the air is cleaner in the country."

You could leave the city, you think. But you don't know if you want to abandon your home.

➤ To flee the city, turn to page **78**.

➤ To stay in your home, turn to page **80**.

The next morning you pack your things and make your way out of the city. You can't believe that just yesterday the city was normal. Today it seems that the world has turned upside down.

Screams and moans fill the air. Rotting bodies lie in the streets. Many are covered with horrible black splotches and stinking, pus-filled buboes. Men called *becchini*, who are paid to take the dead away, carry stretchers piled with several bodies. The city bells no longer chime.

You make it out of the city and head for the countryside. There is no one else on the road, and the quiet is frightening. You are astonished to see farm animals, dogs, and even fine horses roaming the roads. Taking one of the horses, you ride until you see a lone farmhouse. Maybe someone there will give you food and shelter for the night.

The farmyard is eerily quiet. The door to the house stands open. The house is comfortably furnished, and you find bread and cheese in the kitchen. You eat your fill, and then find a bed upstairs. By now you are tired and stiff, with chills and a fever. As you fall asleep, you don't know that you have been infected with the plague. You die before morning.

THE END

To follow another path, turn to page 11.
To read the conclusion, turn to page 101.

79

"I don't think it will be better in the country," you say. "There are no doctors in the small villages, and the people there suffer greatly."

"Good luck, friend," Giovanni says. "I am staying too. I will write about this terrible plague, if I survive." You hug, and he leaves.

After the plague, Giovanni Boccaccio wrote a book called *The Decameron*. The book describes what the plague was like.

You look out your window and can't believe what you see. Bodies lie in the streets. You recognize their faces. They were your friends and neighbors. As you watch, two pigs wander down the street. At first this is a funny sight — who imagines seeing pigs walking down the street alone? They begin rooting through the rumpled clothing of the dead. In no time, the pigs begin shaking as if they were poisoned. Then they drop dead.

Turn the page.

You are terrified now. This sickness is everywhere. God must be punishing people for their terrible sins. You've heard that the poison is spread through the air. If you breathe in the poison, it will harm your body. You think that the only thing that could possibly save you is to stay in your house. But that doesn't seem like a perfect answer either. You have to go out sometime.

→ *To take the risk and go outside, go to page* **83**.

→ *To lock yourself in your house, turn to page* **86**.

"If God plans for me to die, I will, no matter where I am," you reason. You wait until evening to venture out. That way, you won't have to see the bodies. Before you leave, you put some strong spices in a small cloth bag. If breathing bad air spreads the plague, this should help. You press the bag against your nose and mouth and breathe through it as you hurry through the streets.

Turn the page.

You're amazed to see a crowd at the alehouse. Everyone is eating and drinking, and laughter fills the air. But there is also a feeling of fear in the room.

You see two of your friends, Marco and Lorenzo. "So you're not dead yet!" they laugh, handing you a filled glass. "Let us drink to the end of the world!"

If having a good time will let you forget the horrors in the street, that is fine with you. You spend the evening feasting and laughing. When the alehouse closes, all three of you go to Lorenzo's house.

The next morning, you wake up to a terrible smell and the sound of moaning. Marco is dead. Lorenzo lies on bloodstained sheets. He looks at you with pleading eyes.

"Friend," he whispers. "Help me."

➺ *To stay and help, turn to page **88**.*

➺ *To leave him to die, turn to page **92**.*

You check your food and supplies. You have enough to last about a week. With some luck, the plague will have passed by then. You settle in to wait.

Two days later, you begin to feel tired. There's a strange tingling sensation in your hands and feet. Then you notice swollen lumps under your armpits and in your groin. Plague!

Doctors tried to pop the pus-filled bumps that formed on those who were sick.

You drag yourself to your bed. There's nothing you can do. No doctor will come. No friend will dare to help you. All you can do is wait for death. And the only way anyone will know that you are dead is when they smell your rotting body, just like all the others.

THE END

To follow another path, turn to page 11.
To read the conclusion, turn to page 101.

You swallow your terror and smile at him. "Of course," you say, as you bring him water. You won't be like the others who abandon their sick friends and family to die alone.

Lorenzo is coughing up blood. People who do that never survive, and you both know it. You do what you can to make him comfortable. A few hours later, he too is dead.

You carefully wrap both bodies in sheets and drag them to the front door. The last thing you want to do is leave your friends' bodies on the street. But finding a priest to help with their burial will be almost impossible. You know that most of the priests are probably dead.

➤ *To leave the bodies on the street, go to page* **89**.

➤ *To look for a priest, turn to page* **96**.

As much as you hate it, you have no choice. You drag your friends' bodies onto the street. As you do this, two dirty-looking men called *becchini* pass by. *Becchini* are lower-class men who are paid to take away the dead. These two are carrying an empty stretcher.

"We'll take those bodies for you," they say. "It will cost you 10 florins."

"That's more money than I make in a month!" you cry.

"We don't care," the *becchini* say. "Take it or leave it."

Turn the page.

You pay the men, and they roughly toss the bodies onto the stretcher and carry it away. The streets are quiet. All the familiar sounds of living — the bustle of people, the clatter of wagon wheels on the street, and the deep chimes of the church bells — are gone. Most of the houses on the street are deserted.

Hundreds of bodies were hauled away each day during the plague.

Nearby a door stands open. "Why not?" you ask yourself as you go in. Inside it is as if the owners had just stepped out for a moment. The table is set with glasses and plates. You wander through the house, taking anything of value.

Somehow you survive the plague. You are one of the lucky few. And now you're surrounded with the things the dead left behind. You move into a beautiful abandoned home, living the life of its former owner. You have become richer than you ever imagined.

THE END

To follow another path, turn to page 11.
To read the conclusion, turn to page 101.

With tears in your eyes, you turn and leave. If you stay, you will surely die as well. It's a miracle you aren't dead already. You quickly make your way home and lock the door. By the time you arrive, you can already feel the swellings beginning under your arms and in your groin.

For four days, you are deathly sick. Once you crawl to the window, hoping someone will see you and help. But you know no one will. The apple-sized swellings under your arms and in your groin turn black and burst, oozing pus and blood. You are so weak that you can't move, so you lie all alone in your stinking, dirty sheets.

You wake up on the fifth day, more hungry and thirsty than you've ever been in your life. Weakly you stand up. You have survived! You find some stale bread and water in the house. As you chew the hard crust of bread, you are amazed that you are alive. It is very rare for anyone to survive the terrible plague. You know that you are one of the lucky few. Maybe the worst is over.

Turn the page.

When you feel stronger, you venture to the window. Everything is quiet — too quiet. The city bells have stopped ringing. There are no sounds in the street. A wind blows mournfully through the empty, silent city. Several bodies lie here and there. Some are half-covered with cloth, and others are not. You get a whiff of the stench of death that fills the city, and you have to step away from the window.

You know others in the city must be suffering alone like you did. Now that you have beaten the plague, you're pretty sure you can't get it again. You leave home and help wherever you can. You know you can't save everyone, but you try to make them more comfortable.

As more people die from the illness, you're thankful to be alive. But you wonder what the world will be like when this is all over.

Huge pits were dug to hold the vast number of dead bodies.

95

THE END

To follow another path, turn to page 11.
To read the conclusion, turn to page 101.

Your friends should have a proper burial, no matter what. You go out to find a priest. At church after church, either the priests are all dead or none will help you. Finally you find an old priest who agrees to help. You hire two *becchini* to carry the bodies. *Becchini* are lower-class men who carry away the dead. You have to pay them 10 florins. That's more than you make in a month. But your friends deserve to be put to rest with respect. The priest carries a cross and leads your small procession through the streets.

At the height of the plague, few people received funerals because there were not enough priests left to do them.

Turn the page.

As you go, another pair of *becchini* carrying a man and a child joins your procession. Two weeping women follow them. Soon after, a boy carrying a baby's body steps in behind you. At first you are very angry. "Let them get their own priest!" you mutter to yourself. Then you realize this may be the closest thing to a holy burial that these poor souls will get.

The priest leads this large group to the nearest graveyard. There he says a short prayer, and you help lower the bodies into the ground. It's not much, but it will have to do.

After the burial, you make your way home.
You try to block out the moans and screams, the
smell of death, and the sight of the piles of bodies
as you pass. At home, you lock yourself inside
and crawl into bed. You don't care anymore if you
die. To you, the world has truly ended.

THE END

To follow another path, turn to page 11.
To read the conclusion, turn to page 101.

Kings and queens ruled over lower-class citizens during the Middle Ages.

CHAPTER 5

The Middle Ages

Historians generally say the Middle Ages started in the year 500. Around the year 476, many things began to change. Nomadic tribes from the north and east moved into the Western Roman Empire. Sometimes these tribes attacked and defeated the Romans. The empire that had ruled for centuries began to crumble. As their government fell apart, people had to focus their attention on survival.

Some people call the beginning of the Middle Ages the Dark Ages. But the time was far from dark. Out of the ruins of the Western Roman Empire came powerful kings, queens, and nobles. A new form of society was created where each person fit into an order. Each order needed the others for survival.

The years between 1050 and 1350 are often called the High Middle Ages. During this time, great cathedrals were built. Universities were founded. Life was full of splendor and plenty for the rich. But the rich depended on the hard work of the poor for food and other goods.

The nine Crusades made up the longest period of war the world had ever seen. In 1272, the last Crusade ended. Thousands of soldiers, both Western and Eastern, had died in the Holy Wars. Christians considered the wars a failure because Jerusalem was back in the hands of the Muslims. But for Muslims, this was victory.

The wars did have one benefit for the Western world. They helped develop Europe's interest in the outside world. The knights who returned to Europe brought home spices, cloth, and foods. They also brought home new ideas about medicine and culture.

The greatest disaster of the Middle Ages began in 1347 when the Black Plague swept across Europe. Millions of people died. Populations of whole towns disappeared overnight. The plague killed kings, nobles, and common people alike. So many people died that there were no peasants to work the fields, craftsmen to make things, or merchants to sell them.

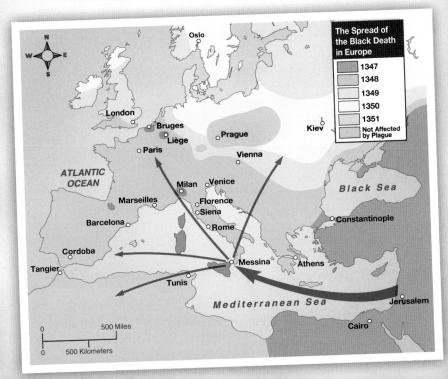

As the survivors recovered from the plague, they began to reshape society. Cities recovered and commerce began again. But there were fewer workers to feed and clothe the rich. The workers now had the opportunity to speak out for better treatment and better pay.

The printing press helped spread new ideas to a large number of people.

Thoughtful people began to question the power of the medieval church and its firm hold on the world. Scientists and artists began to study the natural world in new and different ways. The invention of the printing press brought books to people who had never had the opportunity to read. Columbus' explorations supplied Europe with the vast natural resources of the New World. What was learned in the Middle Ages created an explosion of art and learning that the world had never seen.

The Middle Ages was one of the most exciting times in history. Even though people suffered through terrible wars and disease, the Middle Ages was also a time of beauty and honor. Many aspects of the Middle Ages have an impact on us even today.

Time Line

476 — The Roman Emperor in the west is defeated. Some historians mark this as the beginning of the Middle Ages. Other historians use the year 500 as the beginning.

1066 — William the Conqueror defeats King Harold II at the Battle of Hastings and becomes king.

1095 — The First Crusade begins. It ends in 1099.

1147 — The Second Crusade begins. It ends in 1149.

1157 — Richard the Lion-Hearted is born.

1180 — Philip II Augustus becomes king of France.

1189 — Richard the Lion-Hearted becomes king of England.
The Third Crusade begins. It ends in 1192.

1191 — King Richard wins great battles in Cyprus and Acre in the Holy Land.

1199 — King Richard is wounded and dies while attacking a castle in Normandy.

1202 — The Fourth Crusade begins. It ends in 1204.

1217 — The Fifth Crusade begins. It ends in 1221.

1228 — The Sixth Crusade begins. It ends in 1229.

1239 — Edward I of England is born.

1241 — Eleanor of Castile is born.

1248 — The Seventh Crusade begins. It ends in 1254.

1254 — Edward I and Eleanor of Castile marry.

1270 — The Eighth Crusade begins. It ends the same year.

1271 — The Ninth Crusade begins. It ends in 1272.

1274 — Edward I returns from Crusade and is crowned King of England.

1337 — The Hundred Years' War, between England and France, begins. It ends in 1453.

1347 — The Black Plague arrives in Europe.

1349 — Italian Giovanni Boccaccio begins writing *The Decameron*; the introduction to the book is the best-known account of the Black Death to this day.

1440 — Johannes Gutenberg invents a printing press.

1492 — Christopher Columbus reaches the New World.

1500 — Some historians mark this year as the end of the Middle Ages and the beginning of the Renaissance.

OTHER PATHS TO EXPLORE

In this book, you've seen how the events experienced by people in the Middle Ages look different from three points of view.

Perspectives on history are as varied as the people who lived it. You can explore other paths on your own to learn more about what happened. Seeing history from many points of view is an important part of understanding it.

Here are some ideas for other Middle Ages points of view to explore:

- Many people lost their entire family in the plague. What would it have been like to live through the plague when all your family had died?

- Most peasants lived in villages and worked for a noble. What would life have been like in a medieval village?

- Of course, children in the Middle Ages did not have TV or video games. What would it have been like to grow up during that time?

READ MORE

Clements, Gillian. *Medieval Castle*. Mankato, Minn.: Sea-to-Sea, 2009.

Currie, Stephen. *Medieval Crusades*. Detroit: Lucent Books, 2009.

Murrell, Deborah. *Weapons*. Pleasantville, N.Y.: Gareth Stevens, 2009.

Whiting, Jim. *Medieval Knights*. Mankato, Minn.: Capstone Press, 2009.

INTERNET SITES

FactHound offers a safe, fun way to find Internet sites related to this book. All of the sites on FactHound have been researched by our staff.

Here's all you do:

Visit *www.facthound.com*

FactHound will fetch the best sites for you!

GLOSSARY

bubo (BYU-bo) — a swelling of a lymph gland, often in the groin

cathedral (kuh-THEE-druhl) — a large and important church

chancellor (CHAN-suh-lur) — a title for the leader of a country

chivalry (SHIV-uhl-ree) — a code of brave and polite behavior that medieval knights were expected to follow

crucifix (KROO-suh-fix) — a representation of Christ on the cross

fiefdom (FEEF-duhm) — land given to a knight or other noble by a king or noble in exchange for military service

noble (NOH-buhl) — a person of wealth and high rank

siege (SEEJ) — a military attack

trapping (TRAP-ing) — a decoration worn by royal horses

trebuchet (tre-byoo-SHET) — a medieval war machine used to throw heavy rocks

Bibliography

Adamson, Melitta Weiss. *Food in Medieval Times.* Westport, Conn.: Greenwood Press, 2004.

Bunson, Matthew E. *Encyclopedia of the Middle Ages.* New York: Facts on File, 1995.

Gies, Joseph, and Frances Gies. *Life in a Medieval Castle.* New York: Crowell, 1974.

Horrox, Rosemary, ed. *The Black Death.* New York: Manchester University Press, 1994.

Medieval Sourcebook
http://www.fordham.edu/halsall/Sbook.html

Nossov, Konstantin. *Ancient and Medieval Siege Weapons: A Fully Illustrated Guide to Siege Weapons and Tactics.* Guilford, Conn.: Lyons Press, 2005.

Parsons, John Carmi. *Eleanor of Castile: Queen and Society in Thirteenth-Century England.* New York: St. Martin's Press, 1995.

Winks, Robin W., and Teofilo F. Ruiz. *Medieval Europe and the World: From Late Antiquity to Modernity, 400–1500.* New York: Oxford University Press, 2005.

Ziegler, Philip. *The Black Death.* London: Collins, 1969.

INDEX